Table of Contents

INTRODUCTION

Crock-Pot is the original designer and manufacturer of the slow cooker – offering three types of slow cooker, each boasting their own unique features and benefits. Discover your skills and talents in the kitchen with our exceptional products at your side, and produce restaurant-quality meals for your friends and family with ease. Enhance the taste and texture of simple, low-cost ingredients with slow cooking, letting the flavors marry together over a matter of hours, without the need for stirring.

What is a Crock pot?

In today's world, time is of the essence. Emphasis is on things being done instantly and this includes our food. But crock pot takes the opposite approach. Instead of zapping the food like a microwave or squishing it together like a pressure cooker, the crock pot lets the food simmer for 4-14 times longer than it would normally take. In short, a crock pot is the reverse of a pressure cooker.

Crock pot has a long and colorful history. Originally made out of clay and stone in prehistoric times and heated on the hearth, the crock pot was an invaluable tool for women who had to juggle a dozen domestic responsibilities at any given moment. It allowed food to be cooked with very low chance of burning. We use almost identical shapes and sizes as those crock pots of the old, except with modern materials and using electricity.

How does a Crock pot work?

After putting the food in, you pour some liquid (stock, wine, water) into the crock pot and turn it on. The crock pot will heat up to 80-90 °C, heating the liquid so it becomes steam, but not the super-heated kind like in pressure cookers. The steam will circulate inside the crock pot, evenly spreading heat over the food. After cooking for several hours (possibly longer if you used lower settings), the food is ready. Crock pots generally have a temperature probe inside, which determines when the food is cooked and automatically lowers the temperature to keep the food warm.

What's the difference between a crock pot and a slow Cooker?

Crock pot is a subtype of slow cooker. On the outside, both crock pot and slow cookers look the same: heating segment, lid and pot. Crock pot was initially specialized for cooking beans, but over time it evolved into crock pot of today that can handle plenty of recipes.

Originally being a brand name, crock pot eventually became a generic name for any kind of slow cooker. To be exact, crock pot today refers to any kind of slow cooker that has a ceramic pot inside the heating unit. Both crock pot and slow cooker share a lot of similarities in design, such as being able to hold food in an airtight fashion inside the pot.

Reasons why you need a crock pot for your Ketogenic diet

Crock pots are a great investment: cheap, reliable, sturdy. Especially when you're about to switch over to Keto diet, a crock pot can save you so much energy that you'll preemptively enter ketosis. Crock pot saves time, so you can get up in the morning, dump food inside, turn it on and head out, knowing that your Keto meal will wait for you, perfectly cooked. If you use some fattier cuts, you'll find the meal doused in fat, just the way the Keto recipe prescribed. Yummy!

There are a few ways you'll need to adapt your recipes if you want to switch over to Keto in crock pots, though. Since crock pots don't allow the liquid to reduce, dishes like sauces won't thicken on their own. Hence, you'll have to use Keto-friendly thickeners, which excludes flour and starch. One option is pork rinds ground in a spice grinder and the other is eggs whisked while hot broth is being added. You can also resort to adding

Xanthan/guar gum, which has a neutral flavor and requires vigorous mixing to avoid it turning into blobs. There's cooking bones and skin, such as chicken feet, until you end up with jelly, or you can slowly add flax meal while mixing.

APPETIZERS

Appetizer Spare Ribs with Avocado Oil (Crock Pot)

Ingredients

- 2 lbs spare ribs
- 2 cups water
- 1 tsp garlic salt, or to taste
- 1 cup avocado oil dressing
- 1 tsp garlic powder
- 1/2 tsp onion powder
- Salt and pepper, to taste

Instructions

1. Season ribs with garlic salt to taste.
2. Place ribs into Crock Pot. Pour water and the rest of ingredients. Cover lid and cook on LOW 6 to 8 hours.
3. When ready, drain it. Adjust salt and pepper to taste.
4. Serve hot.

Servings: 6

Cooking Times
Total Time: 6 hours

Nutrition Facts
Serving size: 1/6 of a recipe (6.5 ounces)
Percent daily values based on the Reference Daily Intake (RDI) for a 2000 calorie diet.
Nutrition information calculated from recipe ingredients.

Amount per Serving
Calories 403,01
Calories From Fat (85%) 342,94
% Daily Value
Total Fat 38,39g 59%
Saturated Fat 8,61g 43%
Cholesterol 69,13mg 23%
Sodium 414,48mg 17%
Potassium 218,04mg 6%
Total Carbohydrates 0,7g <1%
Fiber 0,25g 1%
Sugar 0,03g
Protein 13,47g 27%

Mediterranean Delicious Meatballs (Crock Pot)

Ingredients

- 2 1/2 lbs. beef, minced
- Parsley finely chopped
- 1 slice of bread
- 1 onion finely chopped
- 2 eggs
- 1/4 cup flour
- 2 Tbsp olive oil
- 1 tsp vinegar
- 1/2 tsp cumin
- 1/4 cup water
- Salt and pepper to taste

Instructions

1. Rub the bread with water and cut it into small pieces
2. In a large bowl mix minced meat with eggs, bread, onion, parsley, salt, pepper and oil.

3. Using clean hands, knead the mixture.
4. Shape the meat mixture into small meatballs.
5. Roll every meatball in flour.
6. Place water in your Crock Pot. Add meatballs and stir gently.
7. Close lid and cook on LOW heat for 5-6 hours.
8. Serve hot or cold.

Servings: 12
Cooking Times
Total Time: 6 hours and 10 minutes

Nutrition Facts
Serving size: 1/12 of a recipe (4.4 ounces)
Percent daily values based on the Reference Daily Intake (RDI) for a 2000 calorie diet.
Nutrition information calculated from recipe ingredients.

Amount per Serving
Calories 300,77
Calories From Fat (69%) 208,82
% Daily Value
Total Fat 22,7g 35%
Saturated Fat 8,45g 42%
Cholesterol 101,88mg 34%
Sodium 88,49mg 4%
Potassium 279,94mg 8%

Total Carbohydrates 4,12g 1%
Fiber 0,3g 1%
Sugar 0,56g
Protein 18,32g 37%

Philadelphia Spinach Dip (Crock Pot)

Ingredients

- 1 cup Philadelphia cream cheese
- 1 cup Parmesan cheese
- 1 cup heavy cream
- 1 can (11 oz) frozen spinach-drained
- 1 clove garlic, minced
- 1 green onion finely chopped
- 1 bell pepper, diced

Instructions

1. Mix all ingredients in a mixing bowl; stir.
2. Transfer cheese-spinach mixture into your Crock Pot.
3. Cover lid and cook on HIGH for 2 hours then on LOW for 10 min.
4. Serve hot or cold.

Servings: 8
Cooking Times
Total Time: 2 hours and 15 minutes

Nutrition Facts

Serving size: 1/8 of a recipe (4.1 ounces)

Percent daily values based on the Reference Daily Intake (RDI) for a 2000 calorie diet.

Nutrition information calculated from recipe ingredients.

Amount per Serving

Calories 232,03

Calories From Fat (70%) 162,25

% Daily Value

Total Fat 18,47g 28%

Saturated Fat 11,2g 56%

Cholesterol 62,76mg 21%

Sodium 483,51mg 20%

Potassium 198,7mg 6%

Total Carbohydrates 5,81g 2%

Fiber 1,67g 7%

Sugar 1,81g

Protein 11,7g 23%

Shredded Pork with Paprika Appetizer (Crock Pot)

Ingredients

- 3 1/4 Tbsp paprika
- 1 tsp cumin powder
- Salt and pepper to taste
- 3 lbs. pork loin
- 2 Tbsp vegetable oil
- 2 green onions, chopped
- 4 Tbsp tomato paste
- 2 cups water
- 1/4 cup wine vinegar
- BBQ sauce to serve (optional)

Instructions

1. Mix paprika, cumin powder, and salt and pepper until well incorporated. Spread the pork with the spice mixture.
2. Heat the oil in a skillet. Add meat and cook until golden brown on all sides.
3. Place the onions in the bottom of the Crock Pot.

4. Place the meat in cooker, and add remaining ingredients, such as tomato paste and vinegar.
5. Cook on LOW heat for 8 hours.
6. When ready, use a fork to chop the meat carefully.
7. Serve.

Servings: 8
Cooking Times
Total Time: 8 hours and 15 minutes

Nutrition Facts
Serving size: 1/8 of a recipe (9 ounces)
Percent daily values based on the Reference Daily Intake (RDI) for a 2000 calorie diet.
Nutrition information calculated from recipe ingredients.

Amount per Serving
Calories 265,12
Calories From Fat (33%) 87,45
% Daily Value
Total Fat 9,78g 15%
Saturated Fat 2,39g 12%
Cholesterol 112,27mg 37%
Sodium 153,35mg 6%
Potassium 823,27mg 24%
Total Carbohydrates 3,46g 1%
Fiber 1,43g 6%

Sugar 1,38g
Protein 38,98g 78%

Triple Cheese Bacon Dip (Crock Pot)

Ingredients

- 1 cup cream cheese, softened
- 8 slices bacon, cooked, chopped
- 3 cup parmesan cheese
- 1 cup Cheddar cheese
- 2-3 green onion chopped

Instructions

1. Lay 8 slices of bacon on the paper towels.
2. Heat in the microwave on high for 4 to 6 minutes. Let cool and chop them.
3. Place all ingredients from the list in mixing bowl; and stir.
4. Transfer the mixture to your Crock pot.
5. Cover lid and cook on LOW for 1 hour -1 1/2 hours.
6. Serve.

Servings: 8
Cooking Times
Total Time: 1 hour and 40 minutes

Nutrition Facts

Serving size: 1/8 of a recipe (3.5 ounces)

Percent daily values based on the Reference Daily Intake (RDI) for a 2000 calorie diet.

Nutrition information calculated from recipe ingredients.

Amount per Serving

Calories 354,72

Calories From Fat (83%) 293,98

% Daily Value

Total Fat 33,01g 51%

Saturated Fat 15g 75%

Cholesterol 76,37mg 25%

Sodium 615mg 26%

Potassium 151,25mg 4%

Total Carbohydrates 2,23g <1%

Fiber 0,1g <1%

Sugar 1,16g

Protein 12,27g 25%

BREAKFAST

"Baked" Creamy Brussels Sprouts (Crock Pot)

Ingredients
- 14 Brussels sprouts
- 2 cloves garlic
- 1/4 cup Parmesan cheese - grated
- 1/2 cup cream cheese
- 2 Tbsp extra virgin olive oil
- 1 tsp Balsamic vinegar
- Salt and pepper to taste

Instructions
1. Rinse your Brussels sprouts in cold water to remove any dust or dirt. Discard the first leaves.
2. Pour oil in your Crock Pot and add Brussels sprouts. Add all remaining ingredients and stir well.

3. Cover and cook on LOW heat for 3-4 hours or HIGH heat for 1-2 hours.
4. Before serving sprinkle with Parmesan or Feta Cheese.
5. Let cheese melt for 2-3 minutes.

Servings: 2
Cooking Times
Total Time: 2 hours and 25 minutes

Nutrition Facts
Serving size: 1/2 of a recipe (6.3 ounces)
Percent daily values based on the Reference Daily Intake (RDI) for a 2000 calorie diet.
Nutrition information calculated from recipe ingredients. One of the recipe's ingredients was not linked. This ingredient is not included in the recipe nutrition data.

Amount per Serving
Calories 228,71
Calories From Fat (61%) 139,14
% Daily Value
Total Fat 15,85g 24%
Saturated Fat 8,95g 45%
Cholesterol 49,28mg 16%
Sodium 332,45mg 14%
Potassium 522,11mg 15%

Total Carbohydrates 8,57g 5%
Fiber 4,4g 18%
Sugar 4,16g
Protein 10,93g 22%

Bacon Chive Muffins (Crock Pot)

Ingredients

- 6 slices bacon or pancetta
- 2 cups almond flour
- 2 tsp baking powder
- 1 1/2 tsp garlic powder
- 4 tsp dried chives
- 1 1/3 cup grated Parmesan cheese
- 1 egg, beaten
- 3/4 cup milk
- 1/2 cup olive oil
- 1/4 tsp salt

Instructions

1. Place the bacon microwave-safe plate. Heat the bacon in microwave on high for 4 to 6 minutes. Let cool and crumble it.
2. In a mixing bowl, combine almond flour, baking powder, salt, garlic powder, chives, cheese and crumbled bacon.

3. In a separate bowl, combine the egg, milk and olive oil.
4. Combine dry ingredients with moisten mixture and stir well.
5. Lightly grease muffin pan. Pour batter in a muffins cups (3/4 of each muffins cup)
6. Place a trivet in the bottom of your Crock Pot.
7. Place over muffins cups, cover and cook on HIGH for 2 hours.
8. Serve hot or cold.

Servings: 12
Cooking Times
Total Time: 2 hours and 15 minutes

Nutrition Facts
Serving size: 1/12 of a recipe (3.5 ounces)
Percent daily values based on the Reference Daily Intake (RDI) for a 2000 calorie diet.
Nutrition information calculated from recipe ingredients.

Amount per Serving
Calories 229,83
Calories From Fat (83%) 190,92
% Daily Value
Total Fat 21,44g 33%
Saturated Fat 6,34g 32%

Cholesterol 39,42mg 13%
Sodium 471,34mg 20%
Potassium 86,37mg 2%
Total Carbohydrates 1,85g <1%
Fiber 0,04g <1%
Sugar 0,9g
Protein 7,58g 15%

Cauliflower and Breakfast Sausages Casseroles (Crock Pot)

Ingredients

- 10 eggs
- 1/4 cup milk
- 1/2 tsp mustard
- 1 head cauliflower, shredded
- 1 lb breakfast sausages
- 1 1/2 cup shredded cheese
- Salt and pepper to taste
- Olive oil

Instructions

1. Whisk together the eggs, milk, mustard, salt, and pepper in a mixing bowl.
2. Grease your Crock Pot slow cooker with olive oil.
3. Place one layer on the bottom, and season with salt and pepper.
4. Place over chopped sausage and cheese. (you can repeat layer many times)
5. Pour the egg mixture over all ingredients.

6. Cover and cook on LOW for 6-7 hours, or until eggs are set.
7. Serve hot.

Servings: 6
Cooking Times
Total Time: 7 hours and 15 minutes

Nutrition Facts
Serving size: 1/6 of a recipe (6.2 ounces)
Percent daily values based on the Reference Daily Intake (RDI) for a 2000 calorie diet.
Nutrition information calculated from recipe ingredients.
Amount per Serving
Calories 324,42
Calories From Fat (50%) 160,59
% Daily Value
Total Fat 18,01g 28%
Saturated Fat 6,96g 35%
Cholesterol 259,93mg 87%
Sodium 988,86mg 41%
Potassium 222,34mg 6%
Total Carbohydrates 7,23g 2%
Fiber 3,08g 12%
Sugar 1,77g
Protein 32,48g 65%

Cheesy Breakfast Spinach and Bacon (Crock Pot)

Ingredients

- 6 organics eggs
- 1 cup baby spinach, packed
- 1 cup shredded Parmesan
- 1/2 cup shredded Cheddar cheese
- 1 cup bacon, crumbled
- 1 cup plain yogurt
- 1/2 tsp thyme
- 1/2 tsp onion powder
- 1/2 tsp garlic powder
- 1/3 cup diced mushrooms
- Salt and ground pepper
- Olive oil

Instructions

1. In a bowl, whisk the eggs, dry herbs and salt and pepper together.

2. Stir in the crumbled bacon, spinach and shredded cheese.
3. Grease the bottom of your Crock Pot with olive oil.
4. Pour eggs mixture into Crock pot, cover and cook on HIGH for about 2 hours.
5. Serve hot

Servings: 6
Cooking Times
Total Time: 2 hours and 5 minutes

Nutrition Facts
Serving size: 1/6 of a recipe (5.9 ounces)
Percent daily values based on the Reference Daily Intake (RDI) for a 2000 calorie diet.
Nutrition information calculated from recipe ingredients.

Amount per Serving
Calories 225,6
Calories From Fat (54%) 122,95
% Daily Value
Total Fat 13,9g 21%
Saturated Fat 7,15g 36%
Cholesterol 215,12mg 72%
Sodium 434,51mg 18%
Potassium 294,32mg 8%
Total Carbohydrates 6,91g 2%

Fiber 0,87g 3%
Sugar 4,32g
Protein 18,44g 37%

Mottled Kale and Feta Frittata (Crock Pot)

Ingredients

- 8 eggs
- 2 cup kale
- 1 large green pepper
- 3 green onion, sliced
- 1/2 cup Feta, crumbled
- 2 tsp olive oil
- Salt and fresh-ground black pepper to taste

Instructions

1. Heat the oil in your Crock Pot and sauté the kale, chopped pepper, green onion for about 2-3 minutes.
2. Beat the eggs in a mixing bowl, pour over other ingredients, and stir.
3. Adjust salt and pepper to taste and sprinkle with crumbled Feta cheese.
4. Cover and cook on LOW for 2 - 3 hours, or until cheese is melted.
5. Serve hot.

Servings: 6
Cooking Times
Total Time: 3 hours and 5 minutes

Nutrition Facts
Serving size: 1/6 of a recipe (4.8 ounces)
Percent daily values based on the Reference Daily Intake (RDI) for a 2000 calorie diet.
Nutrition information calculated from recipe ingredients.

Amount per Serving
Calories 160,1
Calories From Fat (60%) 95,58
% Daily Value
Total Fat 10,71g 16%
Saturated Fat 4,2g 21%
Cholesterol 259,13mg 86%
Sodium 245,78mg 10%
Potassium 263,49mg 8%
Total Carbohydrates 4,92g 2%
Fiber 1,06g 4%
Sugar 1,52g
Protein 11,24g 22%

S W E E T S

"Pumpkin Pie" with Almond Meal (Crock Pot)

Ingredients

- 1 3/4 cups almond meal (or ground almond)
- 4 Tbsp coconut oil
- 2 cups pure pumpkin
- 1 tsp pumpkin pie spice
- 1 cup natural sweetener of your choice, to taste
- 3 eggs
- 1 1/4 tsp baking soda
- 1 1/4 tsp baking powder
- 1/2 tsp ground cloves
- 1 tsp ground cinnamon
- Salt to taste

Instructions

1. In a bowl, beat together coconut oil and sweetener.

2. Add the eggs and whisk until thoroughly combined.
3. Add the pumpkin and combine spices, almond flour, baking soda, baking powder, and salt.
4. Pour batter into greased baking dish and place into your Crock Pot.
5. Cover lid and cook on HIGH for 3 hours.
6. When ready, let cool and serve.

Servings: 8
Cooking Times
Total Time: 3 hours and 15 minutes

Nutrition Facts
Serving size: 1/8 of a recipe (2.8 ounces)
Percent daily values based on the Reference Daily Intake (RDI) for a 2000 calorie diet.
Nutrition information calculated from recipe ingredients.

Amount per Serving
Calories 233,2
Calories From Fat (64%) 148,1
% Daily Value
Total Fat 17,36g 27%
Saturated Fat 7,15g 36%
Cholesterol 69,75mg 23%
Sodium 354,61mg 15%
Potassium 237,81mg 7%

Total Carbohydrates 9,41g 5%
Fiber 2,4g 10%
Sugar 6,59g
Protein 6,6g 13%

Exotic Citrus Cake (Crock Pot)

Ingredients

- 1/2 cup almond flour (or Psyllium Husk)
- 1/2 Tbsp orange rind, grated
- 1 1/2 Tbs lemon rind, grated
- 1 1/2 Tbs lime rind, grated
- 1 Tbsp grapefruit juice (freshly squeezed)
- 3 Tbs lemon juice (freshly squeezed)
- 3 Tbs lime juice (freshly squeezed)
- 3 egg yolks
- 4 egg whites
- 1 1/2 cup almond milk
- 1 cup butter softened
- 1 1/2 cup sweetener

Instructions

1. In a bowl, beat butter and sweetener. Mix in flour and stir well.
2. Add the lemon, lime rinds, orange rind, and all citrus juices.

3. Whisk egg yolks and milk in a bowl; pour in a flour mixture and stir well.
4. In separate bowl, beat egg whites until they form stiff peaks, then fold into the batter; stir.
5. Spoon the mixture into a lightly greased, heat-proof bowl/dish and cover with aluminum foil.
6. Pour one cup of water in your Crock Pot and place a batter dish.
7. Cover and cook on LOW for 5-6 hours.
8. Serve.

Servings: 10
Cooking Times
Total Time: 6 hours

Nutrition Facts
Serving size: 1/10 of a recipe (4,3 ounces)
Percent daily values based on the Reference Daily Intake (RDI) for a 2000 calorie diet.
Nutrition information calculated from recipe ingredients.
Amount per Serving
Calories 269,63
Calories From Fat (67%) 180,71
% Daily Value
Total Fat 20,5g 32%
Saturated Fat 12,6g 63%
Cholesterol 105,77mg 35%

Potassium 102,9mg 3%
Total Carbohydrates 18,32g 6%
Fiber 0,08g <1%
Sugar 16,01g
Protein 4,08g 8%

Total Coconut Cake (Crock Pot)

Ingredients

- 1/2 cup of coconut oil
- 1/2 cup of butter
- 2 1/4 cup of coconut flour
- 1/2 cup Coconut milk
- 1 cup of sweetener, powder
- 3 eggs
- 1 tsp Baking powder
- Pinch of salt

Instructions

1. Mix sweetener, coconut oil and butter in a large bowl with mixer. Add eggs one by one, and stir well after each egg.
2. Mix the flour, baking powder and salt in a bowl. Gradually, add the coconut milk, combine with the butter mixture until the flour is just mixed.
3. Grease with butter the ceramic cooker in your Crock Pot and line with baking paper.

4. Spread dough evenly on baking paper.
5. Cover lid, and put a few layers of kitchen paper on the lid to absorb moisture.
6. Cook on HIGH about 1 – 1 ½ hours.
7. When ready, open the lid and take out the ceramic cooker. Let cool for 5-10 minutes.
8. Carefully pour the cake out of the mold and let it cool for about 1 hour.
9. Serve.

Servings: 8
Cooking Times
Total Time: 1 hour and 50 minutes

Nutrition Facts
Serving size: 1/8 of a recipe (4.8 ounces)
Percent daily values based on the Reference Daily Intake (RDI) for a 2000 calorie diet.
Nutrition information calculated from recipe ingredients.

Amount per Serving
Calories 308,58
Calories From Fat (85%) 261,86
% Daily Value
Total Fat 30,17g 46%
Saturated Fat 22,55g 113%
Cholesterol 100,25mg 33%

Sodium 161,81mg 7%
Potassium 233,16mg 7%
Total Carbohydrates 8,32g 3%
Fiber 0,74g 3%
Sugar 6,08g
Protein 3,32g 7%

Walnuts and Almond Muffins (Crock Pot)

Ingredients

- 1 cup Almond Flour
- 1/2 cup Flaxseed
- 3/4 cup walnuts, chopped
- 1/2 cup coconut Oil
- 2 eggs
- 1/4 cup sweetener
- 2 tsp Vanilla extract
- 1/2 tsp baking Soda
- 1/4 tsp Liquid Stevia

Instructions

1. Place all ingredients from the list in a mixer bowl, and beat until make homogeneous mixture.
2. Spoon batter into your silicon muffin pans. Sprinkle with finely chopped walnuts.
3. Place inside of the Crock pot, right on the bottom of the ceramic bottom.
4. Close lid and cook for about1 hour.
5. Serve hot or cold.

Servings: 8
Cooking Times
Total Time: 1 hour and 10 minutes

Nutrition Facts
Serving size: 1/8 of a recipe (2.5 ounces)
Percent daily values based on the Reference Daily Intake (RDI) for a 2000 calorie diet.
Nutrition information calculated from recipe ingredients.

Amount per Serving
Calories 384
Calories From Fat (77%) 297,33
% Daily Value
Total Fat 35,03g 54%
Saturated Fat 13,9g 70%
Cholesterol 46,5mg 16%
Sodium 100,16mg 4%
Potassium 269,16mg 8%
Total Carbohydrates 12,88g 4%
Fiber 5,26g 21%
Sugar 5,72g
Protein 8,76g 18%

Wild Rice Almond Cream (Crock Pot)

Ingredients

- 3/4 cup wild rice
- 3 cups of almond milk
- 1 cup water
- 4 Tbsp sweetener
- 1 tsp butter
- 1 Tbsp vanilla extract

Instructions

1. Rinse wild rice a few times with tap water and drain.
2. Pour all the ingredients from your list into Crock Pot.
3. Close lid and boil on HIGH 2 1/2 to 3 hours. Stir every 30 minutes.
4. Ladle rice into a serving dish or small portions and allow it to cool for about one hour.
5. Serve.

Servings: 4

Cooking Times
Total Time: 3 hours and 5 minutes

Nutrition Facts
Serving size: 1/4 of a recipe (7.2 ounces)
Percent daily values based on the Reference Daily Intake (RDI) for a 2000 calorie diet.
Nutrition information calculated from recipe ingredients.

Amount per Serving
Calories 126,54
Calories From Fat (9%) 11,16
% Daily Value
Total Fat 1,29g 2%
Saturated Fat 0,65g 3%
Cholesterol 2,54mg <1%
Sodium 6,08mg <1%
Potassium 134,4mg 4%
Total Carbohydrates 23,27g 8%
Fiber 1,86g 7%
Sugar 1,51g
Protein 4,44g 9%

MAIN DISH/MEAL

Aromatic and Herbed Chicken Drumstick (Crock Pot)

Ingredients
- 6 chicken drumsticks
- 1/3 cup onion, finely chopped
- 1 can (6 oz) tomatoes
- 1 tsp olive oil
- 2 cloves garlic
- 1/3 cup dry white wine
- 1 tsp dried thyme
- 1/4 tsp dried tarragon
- Dried basil leaves
- 1/4 tsp crushed red pepper
- Salt

Instructions
1. Heat oil in large frying skillet over medium-high heat. Add chicken and brown about 6-7 minutes.
2. Place chicken in your Crock Pot.

3. Add garlic and onion to frying pan and sauté 2 minutes occasional stirring.
4. Add wine, tomatoes and remove from heat.
5. Slowly stir in all remaining ingredients; give a good stir.
6. Pour tomato mixture over chicken in your Crock Pot. Cover and cook on LOW for 5 hours.
7. Serve hot.

Servings: 4
Cooking Times
Total Time: 5 hours and 15 minutes

Nutrition Facts
Serving size: 1/4 of a recipe (7.2 ounces)
Percent daily values based on the Reference Daily Intake (RDI) for a 2000 calorie diet.
Nutrition information calculated from recipe ingredients.

Amount per Serving
Calories 174,41
Calories From Fat (27%) 47,8
% Daily Value
Total Fat 5,34g 8%
Saturated Fat 1,22g 6%
Cholesterol 85,91mg 29%
Sodium 231,88mg 10%

Potassium 413,51mg 12%
Total Carbohydrates 6,42g 2%
Fiber 0,95g 4%
Sugar 3,01g
Protein 21,22g 42%

Beef and Mushrooms Stew (Crock Pot)

Ingredients

- 1 lb lean stew beef, cubed
- 8 oz fresh mushrooms, chopped
- 1 cup green beans
- 2 carrots, sliced
- 1 sweet potatoes, cubed
- 1 cup water
- 1/2 cup white wine
- 1 scallion, chopped
- 4 cloves garlic, minced
- 2 Tbsp instant tapioca
- Salt and freshly ground black pepper, to taste
- Non stick cooking spray

Instructions

1. Grease the bottom of your Crock Pot with non-stick cooking spray.
2. Place all ingredients from the list (except green beans and mushrooms) in your Crock Pot.
3. Cover lid and cook on LOW for 7 hours.

4. When ready, open the Crock Pot and add mushrooms and green beans.
5. Close the lid and cook for two hours more.
6. Serve hot.

Servings: 6
Cooking Times
Total Time: 7 hours
Nutrition Facts
Serving size: 1/6 of a recipe (10 ounces)
Percent daily values based on the Reference Daily Intake (RDI) for a 2000 calorie diet.
Nutrition information calculated from recipe ingredients.
Amount per Serving
Calories 224,49
Calories From Fat (22%) 48,47
% Daily Value
Total Fat 5,41g 8%
Saturated Fat 2,23g 11%
Cholesterol 74,84mg 25%
Sodium 75,41mg 3%
Potassium 538,2mg 15%
Total Carbohydrates 12,25g 4%
Fiber 2,03g 8%
Sugar 3,4g
Protein 26,77g 54%

Bretagne Beef and Zucchini Stew (Slow Cooker)

Ingredients

- 1 1/2 lbs stew beef
- 1 cup diced tomatoes
- 3 cups zucchini, chopped
- 1 can (6 oz) green chili pepper, drained
- 1 onion, chopped
- 4 cloves garlic, minced
- 4 Tbsp almond flour
- 1 Tbsp dried oregano
- 2 tsp ground cumin
- Ground red pepper
- Salt to taste

Instructions

1. Combine all ingredients (except flour) in your Crock Pot and stir well.

2. Cover lid and cook on LOW settings for 7 to 8 hours, or until meat is tender.
3. Turn to HIGH setting and stir in almond flour; stir well.
4. Cover and cook on HIGH for 20-25 minutes more.
5. Serve hot.

Servings: 6
Cooking Times
Total Time: 8 hours

Nutrition Facts
Serving size: 1/6 of a recipe (8.5 ounces)
Percent daily values based on the Reference Daily Intake (RDI) for a 2000 calorie diet.
Nutrition information calculated from recipe ingredients.
Amount per Serving
Calories 160,44
Calories From Fat (28%) 44,87
% Daily Value
Total Fat 5,03g 8%
Saturated Fat 2,05g 10%
Cholesterol 59,54mg 20%
Sodium 176,53mg 7%
Potassium 683,22mg 20%
Total Carbohydrates 8,18g 3%
Fiber 2,01g 8%

Sugar 4,1g
Protein 22,09g 44%

Lamb Stew with Peas and Thyme (Crock Pot)

Ingredients

- 1 1/4 lb lamb chops
- 1 1/4 cup water
- 1 cup green peas
- 2 ribs celery
- 2 green bell peppers
- 1 sweet potato, quartered
- 1 carrot, sliced
- 1 onion, quartered
- 3 Tbsp cold water
- 1 1/2 Tbsp almond flour
- 2 Tbsp chopped thyme
- Salt and fresh pepper to taste

Instructions

1. Place the lamb chops in your Crock Pot, and barely cover with 1 ¼ cups water.
2. Add carrots, celery, green pepper, salt and pepper.
3. Cover lid and simmer on LOW for 6 hours.

4. Open the lid and stir in the peas, almond flour and water mixture. Stir until stew is thickened.
5. Cover and cook for 1 - 1/2 hour on LOW setting.
6. Sprinkle fresh thyme, adjust seasonings and serve.

Servings: 5

Cooking Times
Total Time: 4 hours
Nutrition Facts
Serving size: 1/5 of a recipe (11.4 ounces)
Percent daily values based on the Reference Daily Intake (RDI) for a 2000 calorie diet.
Nutrition information calculated from recipe ingredients.
Amount per Serving
Calories 318,18
Calories From Fat (47%) 150,09
% Daily Value
Total Fat 16,66g 26%
Saturated Fat 7,9g 40%
Cholesterol 74,84mg 25%
Sodium 86,05mg 4%
Potassium 702,02mg 20%
Total Carbohydrates 8,14g 5%
Fiber 5,92g 24%
Sugar 4,47g
Protein 25,62g 51%

Marinated Goat or Lamb Curry (Crock Pot)

Ingredients
Marinade

- 1 lb of goat or lamb
- Juice of 1 lemon
- 2 Tbsp curry powder
- 3 cloves of garlic, finely chopped
- 1 large piece of fresh ginger root, peeled and finely chopped
- 1 medium onion, finely chopped

Curry

- 2 Tbsp peanut oil
- 1 Tbsp almond flour
- 2 red onions cut into rings
- 1 cup of cauliflower
- 1 red chilli, seeds removed and finely chopped
- 1 Tbsp curry powder
- 1 cup chopped tomatoes
- 1 1/4 cup coconut milk

- Salt and pepper to taste

Instructions

1. Wash, dry and wrap the meat with kitchen roll, and place in a large bowl.
2. Sprinkle with lemon juice and curry powder, garlic, ginger and chopped onion.
3. Cover bowl with foil and marinate overnight in refrigerator.
4. Heat the oil in a large frying pan and brow marinated drained meat for 2 to 3 minutes.
5. Then, add the remaining marinade from the bowl and 1 tablespoon of flour and cook for one minute.
6. Add meat to your Crock Pot.
7. Add the onion, cauliflower, red chili, curry powder, tomatoes and the coconut milk. Adjust salt and pepper.
8. Close lid and cook on HIGH for 5 hours, or on LOW 6 - 8 hours.
9. Serve hot.

Servings: 6
Cooking Times
Total Time: 8 hours and 5 minutes

Nutrition Facts
Serving size: 1/6 of a recipe (10.2 ounces)

Percent daily values based on the Reference Daily Intake (RDI) for a 2000 calorie diet.
Nutrition information calculated from recipe ingredients.

Amount per Serving
Calories 352,85
Calories From Fat (65%) 230,53

% Daily Value
Total Fat 26,52g 41%
Saturated Fat 14,54g 73%
Cholesterol 50,65mg 17%
Sodium 166,04mg 7%
Potassium 599,88mg 17%
Total Carbohydrates 14,34g 5%
Fiber 3,32g 13%
Sugar 3,15g
Protein 17,2g 34%

Minced Meat & Vegetable Curry (Crock Pot)

Ingredients

- 1/2 lb minced beef
- 3 zucchini, thinly sliced
- 2 cup water
- 2 sweet potatoes
- 1 onion, chopped
- 2 carrots, sliced
- 1 can of whole tomatoes
- 2 celery slices, sliced
- 1 red peppers, chopped
- 1 tsp chili powder
- 1 green chili peppers, chopped
- 2 cloves of garlic, finely chopped
- 1 Tbsp dried oregano
- 2 tsp of ground cumin
- Olive oil

- Salt to taste

Instructions

1. In a small pot heat the oil, and sauté minced meat for two-three minutes.
2. Place all ingredients (including minced meat) from the list into Crock Pot and stir well.
3. Cover lid and cook on HIGH 3-4 hours or on LOW for 6-8 hours.
4. Serve hot.

Servings: 6
Cooking Times
Total Time: 6 hours

Nutrition Facts
Serving size: 1/6 of a recipe (15 ounces)
Percent daily values based on the Reference Daily Intake (RDI) for a 2000 calorie diet.
Nutrition information calculated from recipe ingredients.

Amount per Serving
Calories 168,39
Calories From Fat (47%) 79,25
% Daily Value
Total Fat 8,63g 13%
Saturated Fat 3,3g 17%
Cholesterol 28,35mg 9%

Sodium 179,26mg 7%
Potassium 768,37mg 22%
Total Carbohydrates 8,49g 5%
Fiber 4,16g 17%
Sugar 5,25g
Protein 9,75g 20%

Pork Chops with Almond Sauce (Crock Pot)

Ingredients

- 6 pork chops
- 4 Tbsp almond flour
- 2 Tbsp vegetable oil
- 2 spring onion, sliced
- 3 cups water
- 2 Tbsp almond flour
- 1 cup salt and pepper to taste
- Whipping cream or sour cream
- Garlic powder
- Parsley (fresh and chopped)

Instructions

1. Season pork chops with salt, pepper and garlic powder.
2. Place almond flour on a plate and roll the chops.
3. Pour some oil in a pan and sauté the chops two-three minutes.
4. Place pork chops in the Crock Pot and cover with onion.

5. Pour the water over the chops, close the lid and cook on LOW 7-8 hours.
6. Remove pork chops from the Crock Pot in a casserole dish and cover with foil. Keep warm.
7. In a small saucepan, mix almond flour with the sour cream; cook over low heat until the sauce is thickened.
8. Pour sauce over pork chops, sprinkle with chopped parsley and serve.

Servings: 6
Cooking Times
Total Time: 8 hours and 25 minutes

Nutrition Facts
Serving size: 1/6 of a recipe (8.1 ounces)
Percent daily values based on the Reference Daily Intake (RDI) for a 2000 calorie diet.
Nutrition information calculated from recipe ingredients.

Amount per Serving
Calories 347,14
Calories From Fat (68%) 235,4
% Daily Value
Total Fat 26,87g 41%
Saturated Fat 11,23g 56%
Cholesterol 115,72mg 39%

Sodium 63,96mg 3%
Potassium 458,27mg 13%
Total Carbohydrates 3,16g 1%
Fiber 1,01g 4%
Sugar 0,67g
Protein 23,51g 47%

Pork Chops in Dark Sauce (Crock Pot)

Ingredients

- 6 Pork chops without bone
- 4 Tbsp brown sweetener as Splenda or Truvia
- 1 tsp ginger powder
- 1/4 cup coconut aminos
- 4 Tbsp ketchup
- 2 cloves of garlic, crushed
- Salt and ground pepper to taste

Instructions

1. Add pork chops to your Crock Pot.
2. In a bowl, whisk remaining ingredients and add over meat; mix well.
3. Close lid and cook at LOW setting for 6 hours.
4. Serve hot.

Servings: 6

Cooking Times

Total Time: 6 hours and 5 minutes

Nutrition Facts

Serving size: 1/6 of a recipe (7.8 ounces)

Percent daily values based on the Reference Daily Intake (RDI) for a 2000 calorie diet.

Nutrition information calculated from recipe ingredients.

Amount per Serving

Calories 256,03

Calories From Fat (23%) 57,65

% Daily Value

Total Fat 6,37g 10%

Saturated Fat 2,24g 11%

Cholesterol 122,1mg 41%

Sodium 556,35mg 23%

Potassium 777,33mg 22%

Total Carbohydrates 4,79g 2%

Fiber 0,14g <1%

Sugar 3,41g

Protein 42,27g 85%

Pork Sausages and Sweet Potato Hash (Crock Pot)

Ingredients

- 12 oz pork sausage
- 3 lbs sweet potatoes
- 2 cups leeks, sliced
- 1 tsp dried thyme leaves
- 1/4 cup water
- 1 cup freshly shredded Parmesan cheese
- Salt and freshly ground black pepper to taste
- Non-sticking cooking spray

Instructions

1. Spray the inner side of your Crock Pot with non-sticking cooking spray.
2. In a frying pan, cook sausage over medium-high heat until no longer pink; drain.
3. Stir chopped leeks and thyme.
4. Place a half of sweet potatoes on the bottom of Crock Pot, sausage mixture and cheese. Repeat with remaining sweet potatoes and sausage mixture.

5. Pour water over top and sprinkle with remaining cheese.
6. Cover lid and cook on HIGH setting FOR 2 1/2 - 3 hours or until sweet potatoes are tender.
7. Serve hot.

Servings: 8
Cooking Times
Total Time: 2 hours and 55 minutes

Nutrition Facts
Serving size: 1/8 of a recipe (9 ounces)
Percent daily values based on the Reference Daily Intake (RDI) for a 2000 calorie diet.
Nutrition information calculated from recipe ingredients.

Amount per Serving
Calories 218,63
Calories From Fat (70%) 152,34
% Daily Value
Total Fat 16,99g 26%
Saturated Fat 6,97g 35%
Cholesterol 43,32mg 14%
Sodium 506,84mg 21%
Potassium 172,52mg 5%
Total Carbohydrates 4,92g 2%
Fiber 0,48g 2%

Sugar 1,73g
Protein 11,22g 22%

Roast Pork with Sweet Potatoes and Thyme (Crock Pot)

Ingredients
- 1 Tbsp vegetable oil
- 2 lbs of roast pork without bone
- 4 sweet potatoes, peeled and quartered
- 1 onion, peeled and quartered
- 6 garlic cloves, peeled
- 2 cup water
- 1 Tbsp fresh thyme
- Salt and pepper to taste

Instructions
1. Heat the oil in a heavy frying pan and sauté the meat seasoned with salt and pepper from all sides.
2. Add the sweet potatoes, the onion and the garlic to the Crock Pot and place over the roasted pork.
3. Add the water and fresh thyme; stir slightly.
4. Cover lid and cook on LOW for 6 hours.

5. Serve hot.

Servings: 4
Cooking Times
Total Time: 6 hours and 15 minutes

Nutrition Facts
Serving size: 1/4 of a recipe (15 ounces)
Percent daily values based on the Reference Daily
Intake (RDI) for a 2000 calorie diet.
Nutrition information calculated from recipe
ingredients.

Amount per Serving
Calories 338,11
Calories From Fat (30%) 101,63
% Daily Value
Total Fat 11,31g 17%
Saturated Fat 3,02g 15%
Cholesterol 149,69mg 50%
Sodium 114,03mg 5%
Potassium 941,9mg 27%
Total Carbohydrates 4,39g 1%
Fiber 0,64g 3%
Sugar 1,34g
Protein 51,46g 103%

Sausages and Bacon with Mushrooms (Crock Pot)

Ingredients

- 6 sausages sliced
- 6 slices of bacon
- 1 carrots, peeled and diced
- 2 leeks, chopped
- 2 Tbsp tomato to taste
- Paprika powder and dried mixed herbs
- 2 Tbsp almond flour
- 1 1/2 cup water
- 2 cups mushrooms, sliced
- Salt and ground pepper to taste

Instructions

1. Place sausage, bacon and vegetables to your Crock Pot.
2. Add tomato paste and stir.

3. In a small bowl mix paprika powder and dried mixed herbs, almond flour, salt and pepper to taste with 2-3 tablespoon of water. Pour the sauce in a Crock Pot.
4. Finally, pour the water and give a good stir.
5. Cover and cook for 3 to 4 hours at HIGH or for 9 hours at LOW temperature.
6. Add the mushrooms 30 minutes before the end of the cooking time.
7. Serve hot.

Servings: 6
Cooking Times
Total Time: 9 hours and 5 minutes
Nutrition Facts
Serving size: 1/6 of a recipe (8.7 ounces)
Percent daily values based on the Reference Daily Intake (RDI) for a 2000 calorie diet.
Nutrition information calculated from recipe ingredients.

Amount per Serving
Calories 399,96
Calories From Fat (75%) 298,03
% Daily Value
Total Fat 33,42g 51%
Saturated Fat 9,82g 49%
Cholesterol 85,57mg 29%

Sodium 846,38mg 35%
Potassium 280,24mg 8%
Total Carbohydrates 8,64g 3%
Fiber 1,51g 6%
Sugar 2,52g
Protein 17,62g 35%

Shredded Pork with Chipotle (Crock Pot)

Ingredients

- 2 1/2 lbs. pork loin
- 1 Tbsp minced garlic
- 2 Tbsp chipotles in adobo sauce
- 1 cup onion (chopped)
- 1/4 cup fresh lime juice
- 2 Tbsp apple cider vinegar
- 3 bay leaves
- 1 Tbsp dried oregano
- 1 Tbsp ground cumin
- 1 tsp pepper
- 1/2 cup water
- Salt and freshly ground pepper to taste

Instructions

1. Place all ingredients from the list in your Crock Pot with pork on the top.

2. Cover lid and cook on HIGH for about 4 hours or on LOW for about 6-8 hours, or until meat is tender and easy to shred.
3. Open lid and discard the bay leaves.
4. Transfer meat to plate and shred.
5. Bring back meat into Crock Pot. Stir, adjust salt and pepper and serve.

Servings: 6
Cooking Times
Total Time: 6 hours

Nutrition Facts
Serving size: 1/6 of a recipe (9 ounces)
Percent daily values based on the Reference Daily Intake (RDI) for a 2000 calorie diet.
Nutrition information calculated from recipe ingredients.

Amount per Serving
Calories 229,66
Calories From Fat (17%) 39,62
% Daily Value
Total Fat 4,42g 7%
Saturated Fat 1,37g 7%
Cholesterol 122,85mg 41%
Sodium 104,53mg 4%
Potassium 847,99mg 24%

Total Carbohydrates 5,19g 2%
Fiber 1,06g 4%
Sugar 1,39g
Protein 40,33g 81%

Soft and Juicy "Roast Pork" (Crock Pot)

Ingredients

- 3 slices of bacon
- 4 lbs pork shoulder with or without bone
- 6 cloves of garlic
- Sea salt to taste

Instructions

1. Cover the bottom of your Crock Pot with bacon slices.
2. Make small cuts in pork shoulder and put in the garlic cloves.
3. Rub generously pork meat with the sea salt.
4. Place pork with the skin side up in your Crock Pot over the bacon slices.
5. Cover and cook for about 8-10 hours at LOW temperature. (The meat should be softened so that it can be tumbled with a fork.)
6. Place the pork on a plate and crumble.

7. Cover with some of the cooking liquid.

Servings: 8
Cooking Times
Total Time: 8 hours and 20 minutes

Nutrition Facts
Serving size: 1/8 of a recipe (8.6 ounces)
Percent daily values based on the Reference Daily Intake (RDI) for a 2000 calorie diet.
Nutrition information calculated from recipe ingredients.
Amount per Serving
Calories 490,47
Calories From Fat (63%) 310,97
% Daily Value
Total Fat 34,46g 53%
Saturated Fat 12g 60%
Cholesterol 150,31mg 50%
Sodium 257,43mg 11%
Potassium 759,89mg 22%
Total Carbohydrates 0,84g <1%
Fiber 0,05g <1%
Sugar 0,02g
Protein 41,3g 83%

Sour Red Cabbage and Apples Mash (Crock Pot)

Ingredients
- 1 red cabbage, coarsely chopped
- 3 scallions, small cut
- 2 tart apples, peeled, chopped
- 1 1/2 cup of water
- 3 Tbsp brown sweetener
- 1/2 cup vinegar
- 4 Tbsp of butter
- Salt to taste

Instructions
1. Pour all the ingredients from list into Crock Pot and stir well.
2. Close lid and cook on LOW 8 - 10 hours, or to HIGH about 3 hours.
3. Serve hot.

Servings: 6
Cooking Times
Total Time: 8 hours

Nutrition Facts
Serving size: 1/6 of a recipe (10 ounces)
Percent daily values based on the Reference Daily Intake (RDI) for a 2000 calorie diet.
Nutrition information calculated from recipe ingredients.

Amount per Serving
Calories 147,69
Calories From Fat (48%) 70,15
% Daily Value
Total Fat 8g 12%
Saturated Fat 4,91g 25%
Cholesterol 20,35mg 7%
Sodium 54,42mg 2%
Potassium 434,26mg 12%
Total Carbohydrates 11,19g 4%
Fiber 4,26g 17%
Sugar 6,41g
Protein 2,39g 5%

Sweet Potato and Chicken Sausage Soup (Crock Pot)

Ingredients
- 6 large sweet potatoes
- 1 lb sausage links (chicken)
- 1 onion, chopped
- 1 cup red wine
- 2 pepper, chopped
- 4 Tbsp tomato sauce
- Olive oil
- 3 cups water
- Salt, pepper and seasoning to taste

Instructions
1. Chop the onion in small cubes.
2. In a greased frying pan sauté the onion until get the golden color, about 5-6 minutes.
3. Add sausages, cubed potatoes, seasonings and salt and pepper to taste. Finally, pour the wine and stir.

4. Place all ingredients in your Crock Pot.
5. Add water to cover all ingredients.
6. Cover and cook on LOW setting 6-7 hours.
7. Add chopped peppers and tomato sauce and cook on LOW for 30 minutes more.
8. Serve hot.

Servings: 6
Cooking Times
Total Time: 7 hours and 35 minutes
Nutrition Facts
Serving size: 1/6 of a recipe (14 ounces)
Percent daily values based on the Reference Daily Intake (RDI) for a 2000 calorie diet.
Nutrition information calculated from recipe ingredients.

Amount per Serving
Calories 126,71
Calories From Fat (14%) 18,1
% Daily Value
Total Fat 2,02g 3%
Saturated Fat 0,99g 5%
Cholesterol 18,33mg 6%
Sodium 790,77mg 33%
Potassium 216,3mg 6%
Total Carbohydrates 8,95g 3%
Fiber 0,52g 2%

Sugar 1,26g
Protein 15,3g 31%

S N A C K S

Crispy Sweet Potatoes with Paprika (Crock Pot)

Ingredients

- 2 medium sweet potatoes
- 1 tsp Cayenne pepper, optional
- 2 Tbsp olive oil
- 1 Tbsp smoked paprika
- 1 Tbsp nutritional yeast, optional
- Salt

Instructions

1. Scrub the skin of the potatoes clean. Wash the sweet potatoes well; peel them off.
2. Then, slice sweet potatoes in wedges.
3. In a bowl, mix the potatoes well with the rest of the ingredients from the list.
4. Grease the bottom of your Crock Pot and place sweet potato wedges.
5. Cover and cook on LOW for about 4 - 4 1/2 hours.
6. Serve hot.

Servings: 4
Cooking Times
Total Time: 4 hours and 45 minutes

Nutrition Facts
Serving size: 1/4 of a recipe (3.2 ounces)
Percent daily values based on the Reference Daily Intake (RDI) for a 2000 calorie diet.
Nutrition information calculated from recipe ingredients.

Amount per Serving
Calories 120,72
Calories From Fat (51%) 61,94
% Daily Value
Total Fat 7,02g 11%
Saturated Fat 0,98g 5%
Cholesterol 0mg 0%
Sodium 37,07mg 2%
Potassium 260,14mg 7%
Total Carbohydrates 9,06g 4%
Fiber 2,57g 10%
Sugar 2,9g
Protein 1,27g 3%

Easy Lemony Artichokes (Crock Pot)

Ingredients
- 4 artichokes
- 3 Tbsp lemon juice
- 2 Tbsp coconut butter, melted
- 1 tsp salt and ground black pepper to taste
- Water

Instructions
1. Wash and trim artichokes. Start by pulling off the outermost leaves until you get down to the lighter yellow leaves. Cut off the top third or so of the artichoke; trim the very bottom of the stem.
2. Mix together salt, melted coconut butter and lemon juice and pour over artichokes.
3. Pour in water to cover artichokes.
4. Cover and cook on LOW 6-8 hours or on HIGH 3-4 hours.
5. Serve.

Servings: 4
Cooking Times
Total Time: 4 hours and 10 minutes

Nutrition Facts
Serving size: 1/4 of a recipe (5.2 ounces)
Percent daily values based on the Reference Daily Intake (RDI) for a 2000 calorie diet.
Nutrition information calculated from recipe ingredients.

Amount per Serving
Calories 113,58
Calories From Fat (46%) 52,48
% Daily Value
Total Fat 5,98g 9%
Saturated Fat 3,7g 19%
Cholesterol 15,27mg 5%
Sodium 702,59mg 29%
Potassium 487,2mg 14%
Total Carbohydrates 8,25g 4%
Fiber 6,95g 28%
Sugar 1,56g
Protein 4,29g 9%

Keto Almond Buns (Crock Pot)

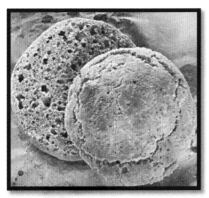

Ingredients

- 3 cup almond flour
- 5 Tbsp butter, unsalted
- 2 eggs
- 11/2 tsp sweetener of your choice (optional)
- 11/2 tsp baking powder

Instructions

1. Combine dry ingredients in a bowl.
2. In a separate bowl, whisk the eggs.
3. Add melted butter to mixture and mix well.
4. Divide almond mixture equally into 6 parts.
5. Grease the bottom of your Crock Pot and place 6 almond buns.
6. Cover and cook on HIGH for 2 to 2 1/2 hours or LOW for 4 to 4 1/2 hours.
7. Serve hot.

Servings: 6

Cooking Times
Total Time: 20 minutes

Nutrition Facts
Serving size: 1/6 of a recipe (1.9 ounces)
Percent daily values based on the Reference Daily Intake (RDI) for a 2000 calorie diet.
Nutrition information calculated from recipe ingredients.
Amount per Serving
Calories 219,35
Calories From Fat (81%) 178,36
% Daily Value
Total Fat 20,7g 32%
Saturated Fat 7,32g 37%
Cholesterol 87,44mg 29%
Sodium 150,31mg 6%
Potassium 145,55mg 4%
Total Carbohydrates 4,59g 2%
Fiber 1,8g 7%
Sugar 1,6g
Protein 6,09g 12%

Parmesan-Almond Zucchini Snack (Crock Pot)

Ingredients

- 2 zucchini, thinly sliced
- 3 eggs, organic
- 1 cup almond flour
- 1 cup ground almonds
- 1 cup Parmesan cheese freshly grated
- 1 tsp dried oregano
- Salt and pepper
- Olive oil

Instructions

1. Wash, clean and slice zucchinis. Salt and dry on a paper towel. Set aside.
2. In a plate, combine ground almonds, Parmesan cheese, oregano and season with salt and pepper to taste and oregano; set aside.
3. In another shallow plate add the almond flour.
4. In a third plate beat eggs, with salt and pepper.

5. Start dipping zucchini rounds in flour, dip into eggs, then dredge in almond mixture, pressing to coat.
6. Pour olive oil in your Crock Pot and place zucchini slices, cover and cook 1 1/2 hours.
7. Serve hot.

Servings: 6
Cooking Times
Total Time: 1 hour and 40 minutes

Nutrition Facts

Serving size: 1/6 of a recipe (5.10ounces)

Percent daily values based on the Reference Daily Intake (RDI) for a 2000 calorie diet.

Nutrition information calculated from recipe ingredients.

Amount per Serving

Calories 303,33

Calories From Fat (68%) 204,81

% Daily Value

Total Fat 24,22g 37%

Saturated Fat 3,61g 18%

Cholesterol 78,01mg 26%

Sodium 160,81mg 7%

Potassium 494,68mg 14%

Total Carbohydrates 11,09g 4%

Fiber 5,23g 21%

Sugar 3,62g

Protein 14,65g 29%

Roasted Parmesan Green Beans (Crock Pot)

Ingredients

2 lbs. fresh green beans, trimmed

2 Tbsp olive oil, or as needed

1 tsp kosher salt and black pepper

1/2 cup Parmesan cheese - grated

Instructions

1. Rinse and pat green beans dry with paper towels if necessary.

2. Drizzle with olive oil and sprinkle with salt and pepper.

3. Use your fingers to coat beans evenly with olive oil and spread them out so they don't overlap.

4. Place green beans in your greased Crock Pot. Generously sprinkle with Parmesan cheese.

5. Cover and cook on HIGH heat setting for 3-4 hours.

6. Serve.

Servings: 8
Cooking Times
Total Time: 4 hours and 5 minutes

Nutrition Facts
Serving size: 1/8 of a recipe (4.4 ounces)
Percent daily values based on the Reference Daily Intake (RDI) for a 2000 calorie diet.
Nutrition information calculated from recipe ingredients.

Amount per Serving
Calories 91,93
Calories From Fat (52%) 47,61
% Daily Value
Total Fat 5,41g 8%
Saturated Fat 1,6g 8%
Cholesterol 5,5mg 2%
Sodium 337,43mg 14%
Potassium 247,12mg 7%
Total Carbohydrates 6,16g 3%
Fiber 3,06g 12%
Sugar 3,75g
Protein 4,48g 9%

SIDE DISH

Irresistible Artichoke and Spinach Mash (Crock Pot)

Ingredients

- 2 cans artichoke hearts, drained and chopped
- 1 1/2 cup frozen spinach, thawed
- 1 cup sour cream
- 3/4 cup Parmesan cheese - grated
- 1/2 cup Feta cheese crumbled
- 1 cup cream cheese
- 2 green onion, diced
- 2 cloves garlic, crushed
- 1/4 tsp freshly ground black pepper

Instructions

1. Place artichoke hearts, spinach and all remaining ingredients from the list into Crock Pot.
2. Stir well until all ingredients are combined. Top with cream cheese.
3. Cover and cook on LOW heat for 2 hours and 15 minutes.

4. Before serving give a good stir.

Servings: 8
Cooking Times
Total Time: 2 hours and 25 minutes

Nutrition Facts
Serving size: 1/8 of a recipe (5.6 ounces)
Percent daily values based on the Reference Daily Intake (RDI) for a 2000 calorie diet.
Nutrition information calculated from recipe ingredients.

Amount per Serving
Calories 258,99
Calories From Fat (69%) 179,22
% Daily Value
Total Fat 20,42g 31%
Saturated Fat 11,93g 60%
Cholesterol 63,44mg 21%
Sodium 436,59mg 18%
Potassium 394,51mg 11%
Total Carbohydrates 8,45g 4%
Fiber 4,07g 16%
Sugar 2,53g
Protein 10g 20%

Piquant Mushrooms (Crock Pot)

Ingredients

- 1 lb fresh mushrooms
- 2 Tbsp ghee / butter /
- Ginger, grated
- 1 onion, chopped
- 2 cloves garlic, chopped
- 1 tsp chili powder
- 1 Tbsp olive oil
- Basil, oregano, thyme, parsley
- 2 cups water
- Salt and black pepper
- 1 fresh lemon juice

Instructions

1. Rinse and slice the mushrooms. Peel and grate the ginger.
2. Place mushrooms and all remaining ingredients from the list into your Crock Pot. Stir in water and stir.

3. Cover lid and cook on LOW heat for 3-4 hours or HIGH heat for 1-2 hours.
4. Before serving sprinkle with chopped parsley and fresh lemon juice.

Servings: 3

Nutrition Facts

Serving size: 1/3 of a recipe (13.2 ounces)

Percent daily values based on the Reference Daily Intake (RDI) for a 2000 calorie diet.

Nutrition information calculated from recipe ingredients.

Amount per Serving

Calories 95,01

Calories From Fat (48%) 45,39

% Daily Value

Total Fat 5,17g 8%

Saturated Fat 0,75g 4%

Cholesterol 0mg 0%

Sodium 21,7mg <1%

Potassium 563,92mg 16%

Total Carbohydrates 7,97g 3%

Fiber 2,42g 10%

Sugar 4,9g

Protein 5,33g 11%

Vegetable Squash Spaghetti (Crock Pot)

Ingredients

- 1 Spaghetti squash (vegetable spaghetti)
- 4 Tbsp olive oil
- 1 3/4 cup of water
- Salt

Instructions

1. Slice squash in half lengthwise and scoop out seeds. Drizzle halves with the olive oil and season with salt.
2. Place squash in your Crock Pot and pour water.
3. Close lid and cook at LOW setting for 4-6 hours.
4. Remove the Squash Spaghetti to the working board and allow cool for 20-30 minutes.
5. Use a fork to scrape out "spaghetti."

Servings: 6
Cooking Times
Total Time: 6 hours

Nutrition Facts

Serving size: 1/6 of a recipe (6.8 ounces)
Percent daily values based on the Reference Daily Intake (RDI) for a 2000 calorie diet.
Nutrition information calculated from recipe ingredients.

Amount per Serving
Calories 130,59
Calories From Fat (62%) 80,51
% Daily Value
Total Fat 9,11g 14%
Saturated Fat 1,27g 6%
Cholesterol 0mg 0%
Sodium 6,79mg <1%
Potassium 399,95mg 11%
Total Carbohydrates 13,26g 4%
Fiber 2,27g 9%
Sugar 2,49g
Protein 1,13g 2%

White Cheese and Green Chilies Dip

Ingredients

- 1 cup cream cheese
- 1 lb White Cheddar, cut into cubes
- 2 Tbsp butter, salted
- 1 can (11 oz) green chilies, drained
- 1 Tbsp pepper flakes, (optional)
- 3 Tbsp milk
- 3 Tbsp water

Instructions

1. Cut the chilies into quarters. Use the knife to cut the quarters into small pieces.
2. Place all ingredients from list (except milk and water) into your Crock Pot.
3. Close lid and cook on HIGH for 30 minutes.
4. Stir the mixture until well combined and then add milk and water; continue to stir until you reach the desired consistency.
5. Close lid and cook for another 15-20 minutes.

6. Let cool and serve.

Servings: 8
Cooking Times
Total Time: 55 minutes

Nutrition Facts
Serving size: 1/8 of a recipe (4 ounces)
Percent daily values based on the Reference Daily Intake (RDI) for a 2000 calorie diet.
Nutrition information calculated from recipe ingredients.

Amount per Serving
Calories 173,76
Calories From Fat (77%) 134,58
% Daily Value
Total Fat 15,16g 23%
Saturated Fat 7,53g 38%
Cholesterol 37,71mg 13%
Sodium 394,08mg 16%
Potassium 309,15mg 9%
Total Carbohydrates 6,67g 2%
Fiber 0,52g 2%
Sugar 2,13g
Protein 2,88g 6%

Wild Rice Pilaf (Crock Pot)

Ingredients

- 2 cup long grain wild rice
- 1 cup whole tomatoes, sliced
- 2 green onion, chopped
- 2 cloves garlic, pressed
- 1 tsp seasonings (thyme, basil, rosemary)
- 4 cups water
- 4 Tbsp olive oil
- 1 lemon, rind, finely grated
- Sea salt and fresh cracked pepper to taste

Instructions

1. Place all ingredients except seasonings in your Crock Pot; give a good stir.
2. Close lid and cook on HIGH for 1 1/2 hours or on LOW for 3 hours.
3. After that time, add seasonings to taste.
4. Sprinkle with lemon rind and serve hot.

Servings: 8
Cooking Times
Total Time: 3 hours and 10 minutes

Nutrition Facts
Serving size: 1/8 of a recipe (6.8 ounces)
Percent daily values based on the Reference Daily Intake (RDI) for a 2000 calorie diet.
Nutrition information calculated from recipe ingredients.

Amount per Serving
Calories 209,81
Calories From Fat (31%) 64,39
% Daily Value
Total Fat 7,31g 11%
Saturated Fat 1,01g 5%
Cholesterol 0mg 0%
Sodium 8,69mg <1%
Potassium 237,85mg 7%
Total Carbohydrates 11,46g 4%
Fiber 2,87g 11%
Sugar 1,75g
Protein 6,22g 12%

SOUPS&STEWS

Beef Stew with Artichokes and Olives (Crock Pot)

Ingredients

- 2 lbs beef meat, diced
- 1 Tbsp vegetable oil
- 1 can of artichoke hearts, drained and halved
- 1 onion, diced
- 4 cloves of garlic, chopped, more to taste
- 4 cups water
- 1/4 cup Ketchup, reduced sugar and low-sodium
- 1/2 cup Kalamata olives pitted and sliced
- 1 tsp dried oregano
- 1 tsp dried parsley
- 1 tsp dried basil
- 1/2 tsp ground cumin
- 1 bay leaf
- Salt and ground pepper to taste

Instructions

1. Heat the oil in a large frying saucepan over medium heat.
2. Brown meat for 2 minutes from all sides.
3. Add meat to your Crock Pot; add artichoke hearts, onions and garlic.
4. Add all remaining ingredients from the list and pour water; stir.
5. Close lid and cook at LOW settings for 7 hours.

Servings: 6
Cooking Times
Total Time: 7 hours and 10 minutes

Nutrition Fact
Serving size: 1/6 of a recipe (13.4 ounces)
Percent daily values based on the Reference Daily Intake (RDI) for a 2000 calorie diet.
Nutrition information calculated from recipe ingredients.
Amount per Serving
Calories 461,9
Calories From Fat (73%) 336,05
% Daily Value
Total Fat 37,31g 57%
Saturated Fat 12,72g 64%
Cholesterol 86,49mg 29%

Potassium 583,86mg 17%
Total Carbohydrates 8,75g 4%
Fiber 4,46g 18%
Sugar 3,18g
Protein 19,02g 38%

Creamy Chicken, Bacon and Mushrooms Stew (Crock Pot)

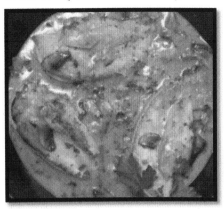

Ingredients

- 1/2 lb chicken breast
- 1/2 lb white mushrooms (chopped)
- 1/2 lb bacon, sliced
- 1/2 cup white wine
- 3/4 cup spring onions, chopped
- 3 garlic cloves, chopped
- 3 sprigs fresh rosemary
- 1 1/2 cup water
- 2 Tbsp almond flour
- 1-2 Tbsp almond milk
- Salt and freshly ground black pepper to taste

Instructions

1. In a frying skillet, cook the bacon over medium-low heat until crisp.
2. When ready, transfer it to your Crock Pot.

3. Sauté chicken over medium-high heat; transfer to the cooker.
4. Pour the wine into the Crock Pot along with mushrooms, green onions, garlic, rosemary, and salt.
5. Cover and cook on LOW setting for 6 hours.
6. In a bowl mix the almond flour with almond milk.
7. Pour over stew and stir a while.
8. Serve hot.

Servings: 6
Cooking Times
Total Time: 6 hours and 20 minutes

Nutrition Facts
Serving size: 1/6 of a recipe (8.4 ounces)
Percent daily values based on the Reference Daily Intake (RDI) for a 2000 calorie diet.
Nutrition information calculated from recipe ingredients.

Amount per Serving
Calories 258,59
Calories From Fat (66%) 170,81
% Daily Value
Total Fat 19,07g 29%
Saturated Fat 5,84g 29%
Cholesterol 48,93mg 16%
Sodium 355,58mg 15%

Potassium 434,33mg 12%
Total Carbohydrates 4,41g 1%
Fiber 1,28g 5%
Sugar 1,58g
Protein 14,01g 28%

Herbed Chicken and Green Chiles Soup (Crock Pot)

Instructions

- 2 chicken breasts boneless
- 1 tsp onion powder
- 1/2 tsp ground cumin
- 1 tsp chili powder
- 1 tsp garlic powder
- 1/2 tsp ground white pepper
- 1/4 tsp cayenne pepper
- 1/2 cup tomato sauce
- 4 ounces green chilies
- 1 cup beans
- 3 cups water
- 1/2 avocado
- 2 Tbsp extra virgin olive oil

Instructions

1. Grease with olive oil the bottom of your Crock Pot and place a chicken.

2. Mix cumin, cayenne pepper, white pepper, salt, garlic, onion & chili powder.
3. Sprinkle evenly over both side of chicken.
4. Place green chili atop the chicken.
5. Finally, pour the water, stir a bit and close the lid.
6. Cook on HIGH for one hour.
7. Open the lid and give a good stir.
8. Close the lid and continue to cook on HIGH for 5 hours more. Serve hot with avocado.

Servings: 8
Cooking Times
Total Time: 6 hours

Nutrition Facts
Serving size: 1/8 of a recipe (13.1 ounces)
Percent daily values based on the Reference Daily Intake (RDI) for a 2000 calorie diet.
Nutrition information calculated from recipe ingredients.
Amount per Serving
Calories 180,02
Calories From Fat (34%) 61,63
% Daily Value
Total Fat 7,04g 11%
Saturated Fat 1,19g 6%
Cholesterol 18,28mg 6%
Sodium 831,99mg 35%

Potassium 599,6mg 17%
Total Carbohydrates 9,82g 4%
Fiber 3,93g 16%
Sugar 1,6g
Protein 13,02g 26%

Light Peas and Mushrooms Soup (Crock Pot)

Ingredients

- 1 cup fresh or frozen peas
- 3 cup Crimini mushrooms, thinly sliced
- 4 cloves garlic, minced
- 2 Tbsp grated fresh ginger
- 4 cups water
- 2 Tbsp tamari (or soy sauce)
- 2 tsp sesame oil
- 1 tsp chili paste
- 2 Tbsp wine vinegar
- Salt and fresh black pepper, to taste

Instructions

1. Place all ingredients in your Crock Pot.
2. Cover and cook on LOW for 7 hours or on HIGH for 4 hours.
3. When ready, sprinkle with grated cheese and serve hot.

Servings: 4

Cooking Times
Total Time: 7 hours and 5 minutes

Nutrition Facts
Serving size: 1/4 of a recipe (13.5 ounces)
Percent daily values based on the Reference Daily Intake (RDI) for a 2000 calorie diet.
Nutrition information calculated from recipe ingredients.

Amount per Serving
Calories 215,83
Calories From Fat (13%) 27,07
% Daily Value
Total Fat 3,11g 5%
Saturated Fat 0,44g 2%
Cholesterol 0mg 0%
Sodium 286,17mg 12%
Potassium 806,92mg 23%
Total Carbohydrates 18g 6%
Fiber 13,47g 54%
Sugar 2,58g
Protein 14,97g 30%

Provençal Chicken, Sausage and Cabbage Stew (Crock Pot)

Ingredients
- 1 lb chicken thighs, boneless, skinless
- 1/2 lb turkey sausage, sliced
- 3 cups mushrooms, sliced
- 2 cups cabbage, coarsely chopped
- 1 carrot, sliced
- 1/2 cup onion, chopped
- Fresh or dry basil
- Fresh or dry thyme
- 2 cloves garlic
- 2 cups water
- Salt and ground black and white pepper

Instructions
1. In your Crock Pot, mix all ingredients from the list starting from chicken and turkey sausages.
2. Cover lid and cook on LOW setting for 6 to 8 hours.
3. Serve hot.

Servings: 6

Cooking Times
Total Time: 6 hours and 20 minutes

Nutrition Facts
Serving size: 1/6 of a recipe (10.6 ounces)
Percent daily values based on the Reference Daily Intake (RDI) for a 2000 calorie diet.
Nutrition information calculated from recipe ingredients.

Amount per Serving
Calories 175,74
Calories From Fat (32%) 57,08
% Daily Value
Total Fat 6,35g 10%
Saturated Fat 2,03g 10%
Cholesterol 74,09mg 25%
Sodium 303,29mg 13%
Potassium 492,63mg 14%
Total Carbohydrates 4,99g 2%
Fiber 1,85g 7%
Sugar 2,09g
Protein 22,79g 46%

Sausage, Chicken and Okra Stew (Crock Pot)

Ingredients
- 1 lb sausage, sliced
- 2 lb chicken breast, boneless and skinless
- 3 1/2 cups water
- 2 tsp peanut oil
- 1 onion (chopped)
- 1 bell pepper
- 1 stalk celery
- 4 cloves garlic, finely chopped
- 2 cups okra, frozen of fresh
- 2 tsp dried seasoning
- 2 bay leaves
- Salt and ground pepper to taste

Instructions
1. In a frying pan heat oil over medium-high heat.
2. Season chicken with salt and pepper and sauté until browned on both sides, about 3-4 minutes.

119

3. Transfer chicken to your Crock Pot.
4. In the same frying pan sauté sliced sausages just for one minute.
5. Transfer sausages to the Crock Pot.
6. Stir in all remaining ingredients from the list and give a good stir.
7. Cover lid and cook on LOW setting 4-5 hours.
8. Transfer chicken to the plate; shred the chicken meat with 2 forks.
9. Discard bay leaves.
10. Return shredded chicken to the cooker and stir well.
11. Serve hot.

Servings: 8
Cooking Times
Total Time: 4 hours and 35 minutes

Nutrition Facts
Serving size: 1/8 of a recipe (12 ounces)
Percent daily values based on the Reference Daily Intake (RDI) for a 2000 calorie diet.
Nutrition information calculated from recipe ingredients.

Amount per Serving
Calories 304,25
Calories From Fat (49%) 149,25
% Daily Value

Total Fat 16,77g 26%
Saturated Fat 4,37g 22%
Cholesterol 139,42mg 46%
Sodium 491,38mg 20%
Potassium 420,13mg 12%
Total Carbohydrates 6,14g 2%
Fiber 1,62g 6%
Sugar 1,83g
Protein 31,84g 64%

Savory Minced Beef and Vegetables Soup (Crock Pot)

Ingredients

- 1 1/2 lbs lean minced meat (beef)
- 1 sweet potato
- 2 sticks of celery, sliced
- 2 green onions, finely sliced
- 3 small carrots, sliced
- 4 Tbsp tomato paste, sugar-free and low sodium
- 1 1/2 cups of water
- Salt and black pepper to taste

Instructions

1. Sauté the mince meat in a large, deep pan over medium-high heat.
2. Drain the fat and set aside.
3. Lay the bottom of your Crock Pot with a layer of potatoes.
4. Then, spread celery, and place over it a layer of minced meat. Season salt and pepper to taste.

5. Add chopped carrots and onions.
6. In a bowl, mix tomato pasta and the water and pour in a Crock Pot over remaining ingredients.
7. Cover and cook at LOW setting for 6-8 hours.
8. Serve hot.

Servings: 6
Cooking Times
Total Time: 8 hours and 15 minutes

Nutrition Facts
Serving size: 1/6 of a recipe (8.2 ounces)
Percent daily values based on the Reference Daily Intake (RDI) for a 2000 calorie diet.
Nutrition information calculated from recipe ingredients.

Amount per Serving
Calories 323.8
Calories from Fat (70%) 226.55
% Daily Value
Total Fat 25,12g 39%
Saturated Fat 9,42g 47%
Cholesterol 64,86mg 22%
Sodium 107,4mg 4%
Potassium 586,28mg 17%
Total Carbohydrates 8,05g 4%
Fiber 2,17g 9%

Sugar 3,29g
Protein 13,35g 27%

Soft Beef with Tamari Sauce (Crock Pot)

Ingredients

- 2 lbs steaks cut into strips
- Garlic powder
- 3 Tbsp Olive oil
- 4 Tbsp of hot water
- 1 onion, finely diced
- 1 small red bell pepper
- 1 small yellow bell pepper
- 1 cup peeled tomatoes with liquid
- 2 Tbsp tamari sauce
- Salt to taste

Instructions

1. Cut the beef into a strips and season with the garlic powder.
2. Heat the oil in a frying pan over medium heat and fry the beef strips. Add meat to your Crock Pot.
3. Add chopped onions, peppers, tomatoes, salt and pepper to taste and stir.

4. Cover and cook on HIGH temperature for 3 - 4 hours or on LOW for 6 - 8 hours.
5. Serve hot.

Servings: 6

Cooking Times

Total Time: 8 hours

Nutrition Facts

Serving size: 1/6 of a recipe (11.3 ounces)

Percent daily values based on the Reference Daily Intake (RDI) for a 2000 calorie diet.

Nutrition information calculated from recipe ingredients.

Amount per Serving

Calories 273,65

Calories From Fat (36%) 98,51

% Daily Value

Total Fat 11,06g 17%

Saturated Fat 2,54g 13%

Cholesterol 83,16mg 28%

Sodium 536,63mg 22%

Potassium 796,28mg 23%

Total Carbohydrates 5,84g 3%

Fiber 2,07g 8%

Sugar 3,36g

Protein 36,8g 74%

Sweet Potato and Sausage Soup (Slow Cooker)

Ingredients
- 8 large sweet potatoes
- 1 lb sausage links (pork or chicken, sweet or spicy, or a mix)
- 1 onion, chopped
- 1 glass red wine
- 2 pepper, chopped
- 4 Tbsp tomato sauce
- Olive oil
- 3 cups water
- Salt, pepper and seasoning to taste

Instructions
1. Chop the onion in small cubes. In a greased frying pan sauté the onion until get the golden color, about 5-6 minutes.
2. Add smoked ham and bacon cut into cubes.

3. Add the cubed potatoes, seasonings and salt and pepper to taste.
4. Pour in the wine. Stir a bit.
5. Place all ingredients in your Slow Cooker.
6. Add the water to cover evenly all ingredients.
7. Cover and cook on LOW 6-7 hours.
8. Add the chopped peppers and tomato sauce and cook on LOW for 30 minutes more.
9. Serve hot.

Servings: 6
Cooking Times
Total Time: 7 hours and 35 minutes
Nutrition Facts
Serving size: 1/6 of a recipe (12.4 ounces)
Percent daily values based on the Reference Daily Intake (RDI) for a 2000 calorie diet.
Nutrition information calculated from recipe ingredients.

Amount per Serving
Calories 126,71
Calories From Fat (14%) 18,1
% Daily Value
Total Fat 2,02g 3%
Saturated Fat 0,99g 5%
Cholesterol 18,33mg 6%
Sodium 787,22mg 33%

Potassium 215,12mg 6%
Total Carbohydrates 6,95g 3%
Fiber 0,52g 2%
Sugar 1,26g
Protein 15,3g 31%

Tangy Spiced Beef Stew (Crock Pot)

Ingredients

- 2 1/4 lbs of beef without bone
- 1 tsp garlic powder
- 1 tsp onion powder
- 1 tsp ginger powder
- 1/2 cup Ketchup, reduced sugar/low sodium
- 2 cups water
- Salt and ground pepper to taste

Instructions

1. Place meat in your Crock Pot.
2. Sprinkle with garlic, ginger and onion powder, season with salt and pepper.
3. Pour the Ketchup over it and give a good stir.
4. Close lid and cook at LOW setting for 6 to 8 hours.
5. Remove meat from the pot and finely chop.
6. Return meat to the pot and cook for one hour more.
7. Serve hot.

Servings: 8

Cooking Times
Total Time: 9 hours

Nutrition Facts
Serving size: 1/8 of a recipe (7.8 ounces)
Percent daily values based on the Reference Daily Intake (RDI) for a 2000 calorie diet.
Nutrition information calculated from recipe ingredients.

Amount per Serving
Calories 353,65
Calories From Fat (69%) 244,43
% Daily Value
Total Fat 26,42g 41%
Saturated Fat 10,61g 53%
Cholesterol 95,68mg 32%
Sodium 257,36mg 11%
Potassium 398,44mg 11%
Total Carbohydrates 4,29g 1%
Fiber 0,13g <1%
Sugar 3,44g
Protein 22,92g 46%

S E A F O O D / F I S H
Clams in Red Vine and Tomato Sauce (Crock Pot)

Ingredients
- 5 lbs clams, rinsed in cold water to remove sand
- 1 cup fresh tomato juice
- 2 Tbsp olive oil
- 2 shallots, sliced thin
- 6 cloves garlic, sliced thin
- 1 1/2 tsp fresh thyme, chopped
- 1 cup red wine
- 2 Tbsp butter
- Kosher salt and smoked paprika

Instructions
1. In your Crock Pot place all ingredients from the list (except clams).
2. Give a good stir and then add the clams.
3. Keep on mind to mix the clams with other ingredients evenly.

4. Cover and cook on HIGH for about 30 - 40 minutes or until clams are tender.
5. Serve.

Servings: 6
Cooking Times
Total Time: 1 hour and 20 minutes

Nutrition Facts
Serving size: 1/6 of a recipe (10.8 ounces)
Percent daily values based on the Reference Daily Intake (RDI) for a 2000 calorie diet.
Nutrition information calculated from recipe ingredients.
Amount per Serving
Calories 267,93
Calories From Fat (30%) 81,28
% Daily Value
Total Fat 9,23g 14%
Saturated Fat 3,19g 16%
Cholesterol 27,18mg 9%
Sodium 365,15mg 15%
Potassium 645,7mg 18%
Total Carbohydrates 14,23g 6%
Fiber 0,84g 3%
Sugar 0,42g
Protein 12,4g 25%

Cod with Herbs & White Wine (Crock Pot)

Ingredients

- 3 cod fish fillets
- 1 tsp fresh rosemary
- 1 lemongrass
- Fresh thyme
- 1 lemon rind
- 1/4 cup white wine
- 1/4 cup water
- 2 Tbsp butter
- Salt and ground pepper to taste
- Parsley, chopped

Instructions

1. Heat the thyme, rosemary, lemongrass, lemon peel, water, white wine and butter in a pot for 2-3 minutes; add the cod.
2. Transfer fish with sauce in a Crock Pot.

3. Cover and cook on HIGH 30-40 minutes, or until fish is soft and flaky.
4. Serve hot with chopped parsley.

Servings: 4
Cooking Times
Total Time: 50 minutes

Nutrition Facts
Serving size: 1/4 of a recipe (8.3 ounces)
Percent daily values based on the Reference Daily Intake (RDI) for a 2000 calorie diet.
Nutrition information calculated from recipe ingredients.

Amount per Serving
Calories 205,77
Calories From Fat (30%) 61,12
% Daily Value
Total Fat 6,92g 11%
Saturated Fat 3,87g 19%
Cholesterol 89,76mg 30%
Sodium 95,61mg 4%
Potassium 730,25mg 21%
Total Carbohydrates 0,63g <1%
Fiber 0,16g <1%
Sugar 0,21g
Protein 30,95g 62%

Hearty Seafood Soup (Crock Pot)

Instructions

- 1 onion, chopped
- 1/2 green bell pepper, chopped
- 2 cloves garlic, minced
- 1 cup diced tomatoes, drained
- 2 Tbsp tomato sauce
- 2 cups water
- 1/4 cup sliced black olives
- 1/2 cup lemon juice
- 1/2 cup dry white wine
- 2 bay leaves
- 1 tsp dried basil
- 1/4 tsp fennel seed, crushed
- 1/8 tsp salt and ground black pepper to taste
- 1 lb cod fillets, cubed
- 1/2 lb medium shrimp - peeled and deveined

Instructions

1. In your Crock Pot place chopped onion, green bell pepper, garlic, tomatoes, water, tomato sauce, olives,

lemon juice, wine, bay leaves, dried basil, fennel seeds, and pepper.

2. Cover, and cook on LOW 4 hours.
3. Open lid and stir in shrimp and cod.
4. Cover and continue cooking for 20 - 30 minutes or until shrimp is ready.
5. Remove and discard bay leaves.
6. Serve hot.

Servings: 8

Nutrition Facts

Serving size: 1/8 of a recipe (9.3 ounces)

Percent daily values based on the Reference Daily Intake (RDI) for a 2000 calorie diet.

Nutrition information calculated from recipe ingredients.

Amount Per Serving

Calories 244,14

Calories From Fat (9%) 22,12

% Daily Value

Total Fat 2,48g 4%

Saturated Fat 0,41g 2%

Cholesterol 157,63mg 53%

Sodium 1467,95mg 61%

Potassium 1045,45mg 30%

Total Carbohydrates 6,36g 2%

Fiber 1,04g 4%

Sugar 3,14g

Protein 44,1g 88%

Salmon filet with Tamari Sauce and Sesame (Crock Pot)

Instructions
- 2 lbs. wild salmon fillets, raw
- 1/4 cup tamari sauce
- 1/2 cup of water
- 1/2 cup wine
- Sesame for sprinkling

Instructions
1. Put the salmon filets in your Crock Pot.
2. In a bowl, mix the tamari sauce with water and wine; pour over the fish.
3. Sprinkle salmon with some sesame seeds.
4. Close lid and cook on HIGH for 30 minutes.
5. Serve hot.

Servings: 6
Cooking Times
Total Time: 35 minutes

Nutrition Facts

Serving size: 1/6 of a recipe (13.6 ounces)
Percent daily values based on the Reference Daily Intake (RDI) for a 2000 calorie diet.
Nutrition information calculated from recipe ingredients.

Amount per Serving

Calories 396,66
Calories From Fat (38%) 190,85
% Daily Value
Total Fat 21,15g 33%
Saturated Fat 3,27g 16%
Cholesterol 183,33mg 61%
Sodium 818,78mg 34%
Potassium 1672,94mg 48%
Total Carbohydrates 1,18g <1%
Fiber 0,1g <1%
Sugar 0,39g
Protein 67,41g 135%

Squid rings, Shrimp with Mustard and Herbs (Crock Pot)

Ingredients

- 3/4 lb rings of squid
- 9 oz shrimps
- 3 fresh onions
- 1/2 cup Olive oil
- 1/2 cup white wine
- 2 Tbsp mustard
- 1 Tbsp fennel seeds
- 1 Tbsp dill
- 1 Tbsp parsley
- 1 Tbsp oregano
- Juice from 1 lemon
- Salt and pepper to taste

Instructions

1. Heat the olive oil in a non-stick pan and sauté the fresh onion.
2. Break the anise seed into the mortar and pour it on the fresh onion.

3. Add squid rings, shrimp, salt and pepper. Pour white wine.
4. After the alcohol evaporates, add the mustard, lemon juice, dry oregano, dill, parsley, mix and serve.
5. Transfer mixture to your Crock Pot, close and cook on LOW for 3-4 hours.
6. Serve.

Servings: 4
Cooking Times
Total Time: 4 hours and 10 minutes

Nutrition Facts
Serving size: 1/4 of a recipe (10.9 ounces)
Percent daily values based on the Reference Daily Intake (RDI) for a 2000 calorie diet.
Nutrition information calculated from recipe ingredients.

Amount per Serving
Calories 436,7
Calories From Fat (60%) 260,82
% Daily Value
Total Fat 29,5g 45%
Saturated Fat 4,19g 21%
Cholesterol 278,54mg 93%
Sodium 495,02mg 21%

Potassium 492,19mg 14%
Total Carbohydrates 7,55g 3%
Fiber 2,91g 12%
Sugar 3,29g
Protein 23,67g 47%

RED MEAT/POULTRY
"Roasted" Pork Chops with Tomato and Fennel (Crock Pot)

Ingredients
- 4 Pork Steaks
- 1 onion cut into thin slices
- 2 cloves of garlic, minced
- 1 fennel in thin slices
- 1 cup chopped tomatoes
- 3/4 cup water
- 2 tsp fresh thyme
- 4 Tbsp olive oil
- Salt and Pepper

Instructions
1. Heat olive oil in frying pan over medium heat.
2. Sauté the onion and fennel for 10 minutes stirring until the vegetables is soften. Add the garlic and stir for one more minute.
3. Add finely chopped tomatoes, water, fresh thyme, and salt and pepper.

4. Once boiled, remove sauce from the heat and transfer it to your Crock Pot.
5. Place pork steaks in sauce and cover them evenly with all sides.
6. Cover and cook on HIGH for about 4 hours.
7. Serve hot.

Servings: 4
Cooking Times
Total Time: 4 hours and 10 minutes

Nutrition Facts
Serving size: 1/4 of a recipe (15.2 ounces)
Percent daily values based on the Reference Daily Intake (RDI) for a 2000 calorie diet.
Nutrition information calculated from recipe ingredients.
Amount per Serving
Calories 580,33
Calories From Fat (65%) 375,76
% Daily Value
Total Fat 41,94g 65%
Saturated Fat 11,77g 59%
Cholesterol 140,62mg 47%
Sodium 304,9mg 13%
Potassium 1012,63mg 29%
Total Carbohydrates 6,74g 3%
Fiber 2,32g 9%

Sugar 4,01g
Protein 41,08g 82%

Roasted Whole Chicken (Crock Pot)

Ingredients
- 1 whole chicken
- 1 lemon zest
- 1 cup of olive oil
- 1 tsp of garlic, minced
- 1 Tbsp water
- 2 Tbsp of mustard
- 3 Tbsp various herbs (parsley, rosemary, oregano, thyme, sage)
- Salt and pepper

Instructions
1. In a small bowl, stir 1 tablespoon of mustard, water, and half the amount of olive oil, the mixture of various herbs, garlic, salt and pepper.
2. With this mixture marinate the chicken.
3. Pour remaining oil in your Crock Pot and place marinated chicken.

4. Cover and cook chicken on LOW for 4-8 hours. (The time will depend on the size of the chicken and your slow cooker.)
5. Serve.

Servings: 8
Cooking Times
Total Time: 8 hours
Nutrition Facts
Serving size: 1/8 of a recipe (7.4 ounces)
Percent daily values based on the Reference Daily Intake (RDI) for a 2000 calorie diet.
Nutrition information calculated from recipe ingredients.
Amount per Serving
Calories 424,08
Calories From Fat (71%) 299,61
% Daily Value
Total Fat 33,39g 51%
Saturated Fat 8,51g 43%
Cholesterol 121,91mg 41%
Sodium 160,81mg 7%
Potassium 334,88mg 10%
Total Carbohydrates 0,48g <1%
Fiber 0,19g <1%
Sugar 0,03g
Protein 28,83g 58%

Sausages and Sweet Potatoes (Crock Pot)

Ingredients

- 12 oz pork sausages, sliced
- 3 sweet potatoes
- 1 cup leeks, sliced
- 1 tsp dried thyme leaves
- 1/4 cup water
- 1 cup freshly shredded Parmesan cheese
- Salt and ground black pepper to taste
- Olive oil

Instructions

1. In a frying skillet, cook sausage over medium-high heat until no longer pink; drain and set aside.
2. Sauté the leeks and thyme for 2-3 minutes; add salt and pepper.
3. Grease the bottom of your Crock Pot with olive oil.
4. Place in leeks and thyme, chopped sweet potatoes, sausage mixture and cheese. Pour the water over top; sprinkle with remaining cheese.

5. Cover; cook on HIGH heat for about 3 hours or until sweet potatoes are tender.
6. Serve hot.

Servings: 6
Cooking Times
Total Time: 3 hours and 15 minutes

Nutrition Facts
Serving size: 1/6 of a recipe (8.8 ounces)
Percent daily values based on the Reference Daily Intake (RDI) for a 2000 calorie diet.
Nutrition information calculated from recipe ingredients.
Amount per Serving
Calories 282,46
Calories From Fat (72%) 202,75
% Daily Value
Total Fat 22,61g 35%
Saturated Fat 9,29g 46%
Cholesterol 57,76mg 19%
Sodium 672,82mg 28%
Potassium 203,32mg 6%
Total Carbohydrates 4,46g 1%
Fiber 0,37g 1%
Sugar 1,73g
Protein 14,74g 29%

Spicy Turkey Burgers (Crock Pot)

Ingredients

- 2 lbs turkey minced
- 1 onion finely chopped
- 2 tsp garlic, minced
- 1 tsp thyme
- 1 tsp red hot paprika powder
- 1 tsp cumin
- 1 tsp coriander
- 2 Tbsp parsley finely chopped
- 3 Tbsp olive oil
- Salt, freshly ground pepper

Instructions

1. Heat the olive oil and sauté the onion with the spices stirring for 3-4 minutes.
2. Combine minced meat together with parsley, thyme, red hot paprika, salt and freshly ground pepper.
3. Knead until the ingredients are mixed well and make thick burgers.

4. Refrigerate for one-two hours.
5. Arrange burgers evenly in the bottom of your Crock Pot (leave space between them).
6. Cover and cook on HIGH heat for 3 hours.
7. Serve hot.

Servings: 6

Cooking Times

Total Time: 3 hours and 15 minutes

Nutrition Facts

Serving size: 1/6 of a recipe (6.9 ounces)

Percent daily values based on the Reference Daily Intake (RDI) for a 2000 calorie diet.

Nutrition information calculated from recipe ingredients.

Amount per Serving

Calories 398,67

Calories From Fat (74%) 296,93

% Daily Value

Total Fat 33,51g 52%

Saturated Fat 8,21g 41%

Cholesterol 108,72mg 36%

Sodium 920,69mg 38%

Potassium 52,53mg 2%

Total Carbohydrates 5,18g 2%

Fiber 0,66g 3%

Sugar 0,9g

Protein 20,97g 42%

Steak with Garlic and Wine Sauce (Crock Pot)

Ingredients

- 4 beef steaks
- 2 garlic head
- 1 cup red dry wine
- 1 tsp fresh basil
- 1 tsp thyme
- 3 Tbsp butter, melted
- Olive oil
- Salt, freshly ground pepper

Instructions

1. In a small bowl mix melted butter, garlic, wine, thyme, chopped basil and salt and pepper.
2. Pour Olive oil in your Crock Pot and place salted beef steaks. Pour the garlic and wine sauce over the steaks evenly.
3. Cover; cook on LOW heat 7 to 9 hours or until beef is tender.
4. Serve hot.

Servings: 4
Cooking Times
Total Time: 8 hours and 5 minutes

Nutrition Facts
Serving size: 1/4 of a recipe (10.1 ounces)
Percent daily values based on the Reference Daily Intake (RDI) for a 2000 calorie diet.
Nutrition information calculated from recipe ingredients.

Amount per Serving
Calories 341,45
Calories From Fat (38%) 128,3
% Daily Value
Total Fat 14,43g 22%
Saturated Fat 7,69g 38%
Cholesterol 140,6mg 47%
Sodium 124,13mg 5%
Potassium 768,56mg 22%
Total Carbohydrates 0,9g <1%
Fiber 0,17g <1%
Sugar 0,03g
Protein 49,63g 99%